EARLY AMERICAN BONSAI:
THE LARZ ANDERSON COLLECTION
OF THE ARNOLD ARBORETUM

PETER DEL TREDICI
ARNOLD ARBORETUM
HARVARD UNIVERSITY

ARNOLD ARBORETUM OF HARVARD UNIVERSITY
125 ARBORWAY, JAMAICA PLAIN, MASSACHUSETTS 02130

The publication of this book was partially funded
by a generous grant from the Arnold Arboretum Associates.
The text originally appeared in *Arnoldia*, Summer 1989.

Library of Congress Catalog Card Number: 89-81096
ISBN 1-878297-00-7

Copyright 1989
by the President and Fellows of Harvard College

This book, set in Trump Medieval typeface, was designed
and printed by the Office of the University Publisher,
Harvard University.

*This book is dedicated to
Constance Tortorici Derderian (1921-1988),
Honorary Curator of the Larz Anderson
Collection from 1969 to 1984 and
an inspiration to her many
friends and students.*

The Larz Anderson Bonsai Collection of the Arnold Arboretum

The practice of growing plants in containers has a long history and is documented in the writing and painting of various ancient civilizations, including the Egyptian, the Hindu, the Greek and the Roman. But it was with the ancient Chinese that the idea of miniaturizing trees for ornamental purposes seems to have originated around A.D. 200. From China, the practice spread to Japan, probably during the Heian Period (782–1185).

During the peaceful and prosperous Tokugawa Period of Japanese history (1603-1867), which began when the seat of the Tokugawa shogunate was moved from Kyoto to Edo (Tokyo), the arts and crafts relating to landscape gardening reached new heights. Many of the great Japanese gardens that still exist today were established during this period, and the cultivation of native Japanese plants, such as azaleas and maples, was a pastime of the wealthy (Harada, 1928).

Growing dwarf plants in containers was popular during the Tokugawa Period, but by modern bonsai standards such specimens would be considered too large and their containers too deep. The styles of the day were distinctive, with the so-called tako or "octopus" shape being particularly common. During the Tokugawa Period, the word *hachi-no-ki*, meaning a "tree in a pot," was used to describe dwarf potted trees. The term *bonsai*, literally meaning "planted in a container," does not seem to have come into wide use until the late 1800's, during the Meiji Period (1867–1912).

In general, *bonsai* is considered an art form, with high aesthetic aspirations, while *hachi-no-ki* is considered primarily decorative in its function. Bonsai styles are characterized by miniaturized trees with natural shapes, growing in shallow trays. Bonsai masters derive their inspiration from nature, and the drastic training techniques they employ are intended to enhance the intrinsic beauty of the plant. Ultimately Japanese bonsai idealizes nature in order to achieve the philosophical goals of truth and beauty.

In common usage in the West, the word bonsai has been popularized to mean any ornamental plant that is dwarfed by means of pruning and by being grown in a small container. It is in this generalized, non-philosophical sense that bonsai will be used throughout the remainder of this article.

The Larz Anderson Collection

The dwarf trees that make up the Larz Anderson Collection were imported into the United States by the Honorable Larz Anderson in 1913, upon his return from serving as ambassador to Japan. While these plants are not the oldest bonsai in the United States, they have probably been under cultivation in North America longer than any other bonsai alive today. To be sure, Japanese bonsai had been imported into the United States prior to 1913,

"A rare specimen of dwarfed Thuja obtusa *(400 years old). A relic of the Tokugawa Era." Illustration from the 1905 catalogue of the Yokohama Nursery Company.*

as evidenced by an auction catalogue from 1904, discovered in the library of the Arnold Arboretum. This sale, sponsored by the "S. M. Japanese Nursery Co." of West Orange, New Jersey, put some 600 plants on the auction block in New York City over a three-day period (May 4, 5, and 6, 1904). Similar events were probably held in other major U.S. cities, such as Boston, with ports actively engaged in trade with the Orient (Long, 1971), but few, if any, of these auction plants seem to have survived the ravages of time.

It is particularly interesting to note that the S.M. Japanese Nursery display of bonsai antedates by five years an exhibit held in London in 1909, which is often described as the first bonsai exhibition outside the Orient (Yoshimura and Halford, 1957; Koreshoff, 1984). Indeed, as far as the author could determine, the date of the first public bonsai display outside Japan occurred in Paris in 1878, during the famous Universal Exposition, thirty-one years before the London exhibition (Carrier, 1889; Maumené, 1902).

Anderson purchased his trees in 1913 from the Yokohama Nursery Company, which was started by the father and son, Uhei and Hamakichi Suzuki.[1] The Yokohama Nursery Company catalogues from 1901 to 1922 are impressive documents, beautifully illustrated with colored plates, line drawings, and photographs. Under the section titled "Dwarf Trees Growing in Jardinieres," the catalogues show pictures of ancient specimens of the hinoki cypress, *Chamaecyparis obtusa*, similar to those that are now part of the Larz Anderson Collection, captioned "Relics of the Tokugawa Era," and provide lengthy instructions on how to care for the plants (see Appendix, p. 36). Exactly how much Anderson paid for his plants is not known, but the 1913–14 edition of the catalogue lists the prices as ranging from one to fifty dollars ("in U.S. gold"). No doubt the older the plant, the greater the cost.

Larz Anderson

Larz Anderson was born in Paris in 1866, while his parents were visiting Europe. Originally from Cincinnati, Ohio, the Andersons traveled to Europe frequently and eventually moved to Washington, D.C. As a boy Larz attended a number of different schools and was tutored privately. Anderson enrolled in Harvard College and graduated in June 1888. Two months later, he set out on a trip around the world. The journey lasted two years and included his first visit to Japan.

After serving in the military and holding a variety of diplomatic posts in Europe, he returned to Japan in 1912 as "Ambassador extraordinary and plenipotentiary." Anderson held this post for only six months, resigning in March 1913, with the change from the Republican Taft administration to the Democratic Wilson administration. This was the last official diplomatic position that Anderson held.

Anderson married Isabel Perkins of Brookline, Massachusetts, in 1897. Isabel seemed to enjoy traveling as much as her diplomat husband did, writing no less than seven travelogues about her experiences. Isabel's family home in Brookline was called "Weld" (her mother's maiden name), and it served as the Anderson's country house during the summer months. As befits a diplomatic couple, the Andersons made Washington, D.C., their primary home.

The part of Brookline where "Weld" was located, in the vicinity of Jamaica Pond, was one of the centers of American horticultural

"Arbor of the Yokohama Nursery Company." Illustration from the 1908 catalogue.

"*Chamaecyparis obtusa* var. nana *Carr.* Genuine dwarf tree about 70 years old. Value 50 yen. Grounds of the Yokohama Nursery Co., June 7, 1918." Photo by E.H. Wilson, N-507, Archives of the Arnold Arboretum.

activity from the early 1800's up until the 1930's. The estates of Col. William Perkins, Thomas Lee, and Francis Parkman, the historian, were showpieces of their time. Later C. S. Sargent, H. H. Richardson, and F. L. Olmsted acquired property in the area, and the Arnold Arboretum was established nearby in 1872. In the now classic 1841 edition of *The Theory and Practice of Landscape Gardening*, Andrew Jackson Downing described the area this way:

The whole of this neighborhood of Brookline is a kind of landscape garden, and there is nothing in America of the sort, so inexpressibly charming as the lanes which lead from one cottage, or villa, to another. No animals are allowed to run at large, and the open gates, with tempting vistas and glimpses under the pendent boughs, give it quite an Arcadian air of rural freedom and enjoyment. These lanes are clothed with a profusion of trees and wild shrubbery, often almost to the carriage tracks, and curve and wind about, in a manner quite bewildering to the stranger who attempts to thread them alone; and there are more hints here for the lover of the pic-

Ambassador and Mrs. Larz Anderson. *Portrait by Philip de Laszlo. Illustration from* Larz Anderson, Letters and Journals of a Diplomat, *edited by Isabel Anderson.*

turesque in lanes than we ever saw assembled together in so small a compass. (pp. 40–41)

"Weld" was famous in horticultural circles long before Anderson became involved in Japanese horticulture. The gardens, designed by Charles A. Platt, were featured in the March 12, 1904, issue of *Town and Country*. The accompanying photographs show a lavishly ornate series of terraces laid out in a formal European style. Following Isabel's death in 1949, "Weld" was donated to the Town of Brookline and is now called Larz Anderson Park, best known for its collection of antique cars. Very little remains of the once glorious gardens.

The Japanese Connection

Larz Anderson's interest in things Japanese predated his assignment as ambassador to that country. In 1907, he built a Japanese garden at "Weld," and before that, in 1889, he

"The bosquet at the end of the garden, the pergola, flower draped, the marble balustrade, the wall fountain and the great Ludovisi jars." Note the parrot in the center of the picture. Illustration from the article on the gardens at Anderson's estate, "Weld," in the March 12, 1904, issue of Town and Country.

Chamaecyparis obtusa *on display at "Weld." Note how wires were used to hold the branches in a horizontal position. Illustration from a* House Beautiful *article that appeared in June 1933.*

brought two dwarf maples back from his first trip to Japan. But it was in 1913 that he became enchanted with bonsai. His journal entry for February 1, 1913, shows this clearly:

> About us were dwarf trees of fantastic shape and stunted plum in fragrant bloom, white and pink, and gnarled trees hundreds of years old with branches blossoming out of seemingly dead trunks in pots of beautiful form and color. Isabel and I stopped so long in this little fairy place that we had to drive like the dickens through the congested streets of endless villages to Yokohama, which we reached without disaster in a little over an hour, in time for one o'clock luncheon. (p. 384)

Anderson must have purchased at least forty plants from the Yokohama Nursery Company shortly after this experience, since he returned to the United States a little more than a month later, on March 6. The purchase of these bonsai marked the start of Anderson's serious commitment to Japanese horticulture. Not only were the plants themselves expensive to import but, once in the United States, they had to be maintained by gardeners knowledgeable in the techniques of bonsai. Given the total lack of such knowledge among Americans of the time, Anderson was forced to hire a succession of Japanese gardeners to take care of the plants. The most famous of them was Rainosuke Awano, who maintained the collection while studying for his doctorate in philosophy at Columbia University.

On at least two occasions, Larz Anderson put his collection on public display: at the 1916 spring flower show of the Massachusetts Horticultural Society, and again in November 1933 when the M.H.S. sponsored a show of chrysanthemums and Japanese dwarf trees. A popular article about the Larz Anderson bonsai collection appeared in the June 1933 edition of *House Beautiful*, featuring photographs of the plants and an interview with Awano. The author's anthropomorphic approach to her subject matter is obvious:

It seems unholy to move such venerable patriarchs from the land where they have lived so long in meditation and repose. But they are here, nevertheless, in this country which was a wilderness when they and their art had reached a high degree of elegance and culture. And on the wide green terrace before the stately Brookline home of Mr. Larz Anderson, noted statesman and scholar, these noble trees, samurai of their realm, seem quite at home. That may be because adaptability is a quality of the nobly born.

Following Anderson's death in April 1937, Isabel Anderson donated the major portion of the collection (thirty plants) to the Arnold Arboretum, along with the funds necessary to build a shade house for their display. This was situated on the grounds of the old Bussey Institution, now occupied by the Massachusetts State Testing Laboratories on the southeastern boundary of the Arboretum.

In 1949, following Isabel Anderson's death, the remaining nine plants in the collection were donated to the Arboretum, including one that the Andersons considered the most special of all, an eighty-year-old hinoki cypress that had been given to them by "The Imperial Household" shortly before they left Japan.

Bonsai at the Arnold Arboretum

Unfortunately, the Larz Anderson Collection did not continue to get the attention of knowledgeable Japanese gardeners following its donation to the Arboretum. The staff did the best it could with its limited knowledge of how to take care of bonsai and the limited financial resources of the Depression era. Additional stress was put on the collection by the practice of periodically forcing it into early growth for the spring flower show of the Mas-

The Larz Anderson Collection of Japanese dwarf trees at the Arnold Arboretum, May 1938. Photo by Donald Wyman, Archives of the Arnold Arboretum.

sachusetts Horticultural Society. While this made for a spectacular display, it seriously weakened the collection and contributed to its general decline (Wyman, 1964). As a result of these factors, the collection shrank from the original thirty-nine plants to twenty-seven in 1962. Included among the casualties was the hinoki that had been the Japanese emperor's gift to the Andersons.

Things began looking up for the collection in 1962 when work on the Charles Stratton Dana Greenhouses of the Arnold Arboretum was completed. This new facility included an attractive hexagonal redwood lath house for displaying the collection during the growing season and a concrete-block cold-storage unit for winter protection. The construction of this building, which maintains temperatures between 33 and 35 degrees Fahrenheit, brought an end to the practice of storing the plants in covered pits and cold frames for the winter. Not only was this practice dangerous to the health of the plants, but the consequent freezing of the root ball cracked many of the original Japanese containers.

Another positive turn of events for the collection occurred in 1969 when Constance Derderian of Watertown, Massachusetts, was made curator. Connie had been teaching courses in bonsai at the Arboretum for several years prior to her appointment, and was well known to the greenhouse staff. Her own words describe how she became involved with the plants:

> Perhaps because I was the only Bostonian who, for almost ten years, had steadily pursued the study of bonsai in the United States and in Japan, in 1969, through the efforts of Mr. Alfred Fordham, Dr. Donald Wyman asked me to repot the Anderson collection of bonsai. I did and began a program to renew the vigor and beauty of these venerable trees. Dr. Richard A. Howard, director, pleased with the initial effort, had me appointed Honorary Curator of the Bonsai Collection.

Working patiently and with a clear sense of purpose, Connie began the long process of revitalizing the collection after years of neglect. She continued to care for the collection until 1984 when her failing health forced her to resign the curatorship. The author, having worked as her apprentice since 1979, became the new curator the year she resigned.

Over the Columbus Day weekend in 1986, a break-in occurred at the bonsai house, and six plants were stolen, including three Japanese maples that were part of the original Larz Anderson Collection. Spurred on by this disaster, the Arnold Arboretum Associates decided to finance a renovation of the deteriorating bonsai house in the spring of 1987, replacing the rotting redwood planks with the more structurally substantial, vertical-grain Douglas fir. New doors were designed that allowed visitors an unobstructed view of the collection. Most importantly, a new security system was installed. The renovations were completed in time for the 1987

Constance Derderian and Hank Goodell repotting one of the Larz Anderson bonsai in 1969. Photo by P. Burns, from the Archives of the Arnold Arboretum.

Illustration of Chamaecyparis obtusa *'Chabo-hiba' from the 1901 catalogue of the Yokohama Nursery Company.*

season, and in June of that year, a ceremony was held dedicating the structure to Mrs. Derderian. She died a year later on September 20, 1988.

As of August 1989, fifteen plants still remain of the original thirty-nine plants in the collection. These include seven hinoki cypresses (*Chamaecyparis obtusa*), four Japanese maples (*Acer palmatum*), one trident maple (*Acer buergerianum*), one higan cherry (*Prunus subhirtella*), one sawara cypress (*Chamaecyparis pisifera* 'Squarrosa'), and one Japanese white pine (*Pinus parviflora*). There can be little doubt that in any list of "ironclad" bonsai, these species ought to be included. The hinokis seem to be the toughest of all in that seven of ten original plants are still alive and healthy. They are also the most ancient and most beautiful plants in the collection. Technically they should probably be considered *hachi-no-ki* rather than true bonsai. According to Anderson's records, the oldest hinoki specimen was started in 1737, making it 252 years old in 1989.

Nomenclature

The one question concerning the Larz Anderson bonsai that has dogged the author for years is the correct identity of the specimens of *Chamaecyparis obtusa*, which make up the major portion of the collection. Are they normal hinokis that have developed their peculiar shape simply as a result of hundreds of years of pruning, or are they a horticultural selection that is genetically dwarf to begin with? Fortunately, the 1901 Yokohama Nursery catalogue contains an absolutely stunning woodblock print of its potted hinoki cypresses, identical to those in the Larz Anderson Collection, captioned "Thuja obtusa var. Chabo-hiba."[2] In this same catalogue, golden and silver variegated varieties of *Chabo-hiba* are offered, which undoubtedly originated as sports of the typical green variety.

Since the name *Chabo-hiba* is not in common use in Japan today, it took some work to uncover its exact meaning. By itself, the word *hiba* means hatchet-shaped (in reference to the foliage) and is the common name for the low-growing conifer *Thujopsis dolobrata* (Kurata, 1971) as well as for various horticultural varieties of *Chamaecyparis obtusa* and *pisifera* (Yoshio and Motoyoshi, 1891; Yoshimura and Halford, 1957). The word *chabo* literally means bantam chicken. In combination, *Chabo-hiba* is best translated as "compact or bantam cypress."

Compounding the problem of the identity of the Larz Anderson hinokis is the fact that they were rigorously pruned for their entire lives. Based on an experiment at the Arnold Arboretum, such cultural practices seem to have affected both the character of their foliage and the orientation of their branches. In 1971 a few cuttings of the Larz Anderson hinokis were rooted in the Arboretum greenhouses. They were grown in the nursery for several years, unpruned, where they retained their dwarf habit, congested foliage, and twisted branches. In 1981, the author planted one of these specimens, which was about 20 centimeters tall and 20 centimeters wide (7 inches x 7 inches), in the Arboretum's dwarf conifer area—to see how it would develop if left unpruned. The plant continued to grow in a manner similar to the old specimens from which it had been taken until 1984, when it suddenly produced an upright leader with looser, less congested foliage. At eighteen years of age in 1989, this unpruned plant is completely upright, a meter and a half tall by a meter wide (60 inches x 39 inches), and has set an abundant crop of "normal" sized cones.[3]

That this is typical behavior for unpruned *Chabo-hiba* is attested to by the fact that in the 1913 edition of the Yokohama Nursery catalogue the listings under *Chabo-hiba* were changed to read, "Thuja obtusa compacta or Chabo-hiba." On a nearby page there is a photo of a narrowly pyramidal evergreen, five to six meters tall (15 to 20 feet) and neatly trimmed, captioned "Thuja obtusa compacta." This confluence of the historical evidence from 1913 and the experimental data from 1989 makes it certain that the appearance of the Larz Anderson hinokis is the result of continual pruning of the genetically compact, pyramidal variety, *Chabo-hiba*.

The earliest use of the name *Chabo-hiba* that this author could uncover is from the three-volume book *Somoku Kihin Kagami*, published in 1827 and reprinted in 1976 with modern Japanese characters and Latin plant names (Kintaro, 1827; Tsukamoto, 1976). This

Chamaecyparis obtusa 'Chabo-hiba' #1100-71. *This plant originated as a cutting from one of the old bonsai plants, but was left unpruned. At eighteen years of age, it is a meter and a half tall by a meter wide (60 in x 39 in).*

work covers hundreds of plants considered highly unusual or very rare. While *Chabo-hiba* itself is not covered, a *Chamaecyparis* cultivar listed as *Chaboyadori*, meaning "bantam's nest," is described. The accompanying illustration shows a plant with two types of foliage, the loose, feathery growth ("Cryptomeria-like") rising out of a "nest" of tight, congested growth ("Chabo-hiba-like"). In the text, the author states that he first noticed the plant as an unusual branch (or sport) on a specimen of *Chabo-hiba*, and propagated it specially.

As this reference in *Somoku Kihin Kagami* indicates, the name *Chabo-hiba* has a long tradition of use in Japan that predates any possible description of the plant by Western botanists. With such priority, 'Chabo-hiba' can be considered a proper cultivar name according to the guidelines laid out in the *International Code of Nomenclature for Cultivated Plants—1980*.

Over the years, three Latin names have been proposed to replace 'Chabo-hiba': *breviramea*,[4] *nana*,[5] and *compacta*. Of the three, only the last describes the plant accurately. Published in 1875 by George Gordon, his description of *compacta* reads: "The leaves and branches of this variety resemble those of the species in every way, except that they are much smaller, and the plant has a very dense and compact habit." However accurate the name *compacta* may be, it suffers from the same drawback that affects all the Latinized botanical names for cultivated plants, namely that it *can be* and *has been* legitimately applied to a variety of plants other than the specimen originally described (Hornibrook, 1938). This lack of precision provides a second reason, priority being the first, for favoring 'Chabo-hiba' as a cultivar name over 'Compacta.'

The historical record leaves little doubt that the Larz Anderson hinokis are best referred to as *Chamaecyparis obtusa* 'Chabo-hiba,' defined here as a compact, slow-growing cultivar with dark green foliage that develops a pyramidal shape over time. Often grown in containers and intensively pruned, it responds to such treatment by producing congested,

"Thuja obtusa compacta." Illustration from the 1914 catalogue of the Yokohama Nursery Company.

planar foliage and contorted, horizontal branches. By restoring the Japanese name 'Chabo-hiba' to the Larz Anderson hinokis, one not only eliminates confusion but also achieves a better sense of their rich history.

Bonsai Maintenance at the Arnold Arboretum

What follows is a general outline of the various procedures used by the staff of the Arnold Arboretum to maintain the Larz Anderson bonsai collection in a healthy condition.

REPOTTING: The smaller the pot, the more frequently the plant needs repotting. This procedure is best done in early spring, mid- to late March, before the plant shows any

"Chamaecyparis obtusa *var.* nana *Carr. Group of trained specimens.* Tsuga diversifolia *Maxim. in center. Grounds of the Yokohama Nursery Co., June 7, 1918." Photo by E.H. Wilson, N-509, Archives of the Arnold Arboretum.*

signs of growth. The plant is removed from its container, and approximately two to three centimeters (one inch, more or less) of roots, plus their attached soil, are removed all around the sides and bottom of the root ball. Any roots thicker than a pencil are cut away to encourage the development of small feeder roots. This process effectively rejuvenates the root system of the plant and prevents lethal "girdling" roots from forming. After the root ball is trimmed, the plant is returned to its original container surrounded by fresh soil. The large hinokis are repotted every four to five years, while the smaller plants are repotted every two to three years.

SOIL MIXES: Plant roots are so intimately involved with soil particles that it is best to think of the soil as part of the plant itself. As such, a great deal of time and care needs to go into its preparation. In general, the potting mix should provide the plant with a balance of water retention and air circulation. Our repotting mixes consist of coarse sand (particle size 1–3 mm), peat moss or leaf mold, and screened loam in various proportions depending upon the plant being grown. In general, we use a mix that is one-half sand, one-quarter loam, and one-quarter peat for the conifers; and one-third sand, one-third peat, and one-third loam for deciduous trees. In either case, small amounts of superphosphate and organic nitrogen fertilizer are added to the soil mix.

PRUNING: There are no universal rules about how much to prune a bonsai; the techniques vary according to the species being worked with. In general the best time to prune is when the plants are producing new growth—in early spring for deciduous plants, such as the cherries and Japanese maples, in mid-spring for pines and spruces, and in early to mid-summer for the junipers and the hinokis. Generally, at least 50 percent of the new growth is removed at the time of pruning. If the plant produces a second flush of leaves later in the growing season, these also require pruning.

- With pines, the number of candles is thinned out by one-half to two-thirds, and those that remain are shortened.
- With spruces and firs, the newly flushing shoots are pinched back to half their length, inducing replacement buds to form at the base of the new growth rather than at the tip.
- With maples, the new shoots are pinched back to a maximum of two pairs of leaves and sometimes only one pair. Any vertical-growing shoots are removed or are wired into a horizontal position.
- With hinokis and junipers, which produce new growth over an extended portion of the growing season rather than in a single flush, the new growth is pinched back several times. If the new growth is not rigorously thinned, it becomes excessively congested and subject to death by self-shading.

WIRING: In young vigorous bonsai, wiring the branches into pendant or horizontal positions with copper or aluminum wire is an extremely important part of the training process. On plants as old as the hinoki cypresses in the Larz Anderson Collection, reorienting their twisted branches with wire is very difficult. These branches thicken so slowly that it may take two or three years for them to produce enough wood to overcome their old orientation. We have found that tying them down with nylon fishing line is more effective than wiring.

For the other plants in the collection, we generally wire young vigorous branches into a horizontal position in order to achieve the effect of age. It is important to remember that wire should not be left on the tree more than a year, since the branch can easily be girdled by the wire.

WATERING: Because the Larz Anderson Collection consists of such large plants in such small pots, their water requirements are quite high. During the period of spring growth, they need watering at least once a day. During the summer, one daily watering is a minimum on days when no rain has fallen, and often they

The bonsai house at the Arnold Arboretum, completed in 1962. Photo by P. Burns, from the Archives of the Arnold Arboretum.

require more than this. Extending this need for daily watering back into the past some two hundred years, one begins to appreciate the magnitude of continuity and commitment that has gone into maintaining these venerable specimens.

To determine if a plant needs water, place the palm of the hand on the soil surface. If any feeling of moisture is detectable, the plant should not be watered. When the root ball is dry to the touch, the plant is watered. It is best to use the palm of the hand to make this determination because it is less heavily calloused, and hence more sensitive, than the fingertips. The root ball of a healthy bonsai behaves like a sponge, that is, water is uniformly distributed throughout its mass at all times, so the moisture content of the surface is essentially the same as that of the base.

When the plants are watered, care is taken not to get the foliage wet, particularly on sunny days when water drops can magnify the energy of the sun sufficiently to produce burn spots on the leaves. At watering time, the pot is filled to the top, and the water is allowed to drain through; the pot is then filled up a second time. This "double dousing" insures that sufficient water is provided to wet the entire root ball and to percolate out the drainage holes. If only the top part of the root ball is moistened, the bottom part will become excessively dry and the plant could be seriously injured. Less frequent, thorough watering is always preferable to frequent light watering for any containerized plant.

FERTILIZING: While the instructions provided by the Yokohama Nursery call for fertilizing the plants with powdered oil cake (consisting of soybean or rapeseed, after the oil has been pressed out) or bone meal, we use a chemical fertilizer solution diluted to a concentration of approximately 0.01 percent

Item #340 from the 1904 auction catalogue of the S.M. Japanese Nursery Company. The description reads: "**Chabo-hiba.** One of the most imposing-looking specimens in this collection. This grand tree once belonged to the famous temple Hongauji, Kyoto, the ancient Capitol of the Japanese Empire. It has been said that owing to its most attractive shape, this specimen was admired by almost a million people, who made the pilgrimage to this noted temple of Buddha. It was trained by the several master gardeners who gave their services to the temple. Trained in the standard Jikka style. Note: its most graceful branches extended into both sides. About 100 years old; height, 2 feet, 6 inches. With Chinese pottery pot on stand."

nitrogen, phosphorus, and potassium. When growth commences in the spring, we water the plants with this dilute fertilizer every one to two weeks until mid-July, at which point we fertilize only once every two to three weeks through October. From this point on, the plants are going dormant, and we stop fertilizing them altogether.

WINTER STORAGE: In the milder parts of the United States, as in much of Japan, bonsai can be left out-of-doors all winter with only minimal protection from the elements. In New England, however, with our more severe winter weather, the plants need to be protected from the cold. A plant that is perfectly hardy growing in the ground is not as hardy when grown in a container above ground. This is due to the fact that the soil, which has great insulating power, never gets as cold as the air, which has no insulating value.

The Arboretum bonsai are stored in a concrete-block structure for the winter. The temperature in the building is maintained between 33 and 36 degrees Fahrenheit, and the plants are checked for water once a week. In general, they need watering about once a

THE LARZ ANDERSON BONSAI COLLECTION INVENTORY

Plants living in 1989, and year started as bonsai:

870-37	*Acer buergerianum*	Trident Maple	1852
872-37	*Acer palmatum*	Japanese Maple	1887
877-37	*Chamaecyparis obtusa* 'Chabo-hiba'	Compact Hinoki Cypress	1737
878-37	*Chamaecyparis obtusa* 'Chabo-hiba'	Compact Hinoki Cypress	1787
879-37	*Chamaecyparis obtusa* 'Chabo-hiba'	Compact Hinoki Cypress	1802
880-37	*Chamaecyparis obtusa* 'Chabo-hiba'	Compact Hinoki Cypress	1832
881-37	*Chamaecyparis obtusa* 'Chabo-hiba'	Compact Hinoki Cypress	1862
889-37	*Prunus subhirtella*	Higan Cherry	1852
899-37	*Chamaecyparis pisifera* 'Squarrosa'	Sawara Moss Cypress	1907
886-49	*Acer palmatum*	Japanese Maple	1887
888-49	*Acer palmatum*	Japanese Maple	1897
889-49	*Acer palmatum*	Japanese Maple	1897
890-49	*Chamaecyparis obtusa* 'Chabo-hiba'	Compact Hinoki Cypress	1832
892-49	*Chamaecyparis obtusa* 'Chabo-hiba'	Compact Hinoki Cypress	1787
893-49	*Pinus parviflora*	Japanese White Pine	1887
101-69	*Chamaecyparis obtusa* 'Chabo-hiba'	Compact Hinoki Cypress	1969

Plants dead or stolen (numbers of individuals of each species in parentheses):

Acer palmatum (5)
Acer palmatum 'Dissectum' (1)
Chamaecyparis obtusa 'Chabo-hiba' (3)
Chamaecyparis pisifera 'Squarrosa' (1)
Cryptomeria japonica (1)
Euonymous fortunei 'Kewensis' (1)
Juniperus rigida (1)
Photinia villosa (2)
Prunus mume (2)
Prunus subhirtella (2)
Punica granatum (1)
Spiraea thunbergii (1)
Thujopsis dolobrata 'Variegata' (1)
Zelkova serrata (2)

month. One must be extremely careful that the plants do not get overly dry during storage as they can become extremely difficult to rewet come spring. On the other hand, if the plants are kept too wet during storage, they become susceptible to fungal infections.

As long as the temperatures remain below 36 degrees, the plants seem to survive, *even in total darkness*. Such dark storage will not work at higher temperatures. The key to successful winter storage is to make sure that the plants are fully dormant before they go in and that they come out before they show any signs of growth. Generally speaking, our plants go into cold storage on Armistice day (November 11) and come out on Patriots' Day (April 19), although a week either way makes little difference.

Endnotes

1. The Suzukis were employed by the Louis Boehmer Company while it was run by Boehmer himself, but in 1889 Alfred Unger became Boehmer's partner and the Suzukis went out on their own to establish the Yokohama Gardeners' Association, and, in 1890, the Yokohama Nursery Company (Unger, 1930; Yokohama Catalogue, 1908).
2. The genus *Chamaecyparis* was established by E. S. Spach in 1842, but it was not universally accepted, and in the older literature it is often treated as *Thuja* or *Retinispora*. Fortunately the species name for the hinoki cypress, *obtusa*, has remained relatively stable since its description by Siebold and Zuccarini in 1844.
3. The horticultural forms of *Chamaecyparis obtusa* are notoriously unstable in their morphology. Specimens of many of the widely grown dwarfs, such as 'Nana Gracilis,' sport out continually, the sport producing foliage much looser than that found on the rest of the plant. When one of these dwarfs produces seeds, the seedlings show a wide range of variability in size, rate of growth, and foliage characteristics (Spingarn, 1978). In the author's own work with seedlings of 'Graciosa,' 'Nana Gracilis,' and 'Verdoon,' they all pass through the developmental process that is normal for the species, first producing a few needle leaves (the juvenile foliage) and then, in their axils, branches consisting of scale leaves (the adult foliage). However, these scale leaves are much smaller and their "internodes" much shorter than is typical for the species, and a congested cone- or bun-shaped plant develops. The length of time that these plants retain their dwarf habit varies greatly, but I suspect that eventually all of them will produce a leader and foliage that are more or less "normal." To put it another way, many of the dwarf forms of *Chamaecyparis obtusa* seem to possess mutations in the genes that regulate the rate of development rather than in the genes that control specific morphological characters.
4. A second Latin name that is often listed as synonymous with 'Chabo-hiba' is var. *breviramea* (Yoshimura and Halford, 1957; Walker, 1976). This curious name was originally published by Maximowicz in 1866 to describe a supposed wild species from southern Japan. Later authors (Masters, 1881; Carrier, 1889; Beissner, 1900) reduced the name to a variety of *obtusa*, but still considered it a wild-growing plant that was cultivated as an ornamental. Rehder (1914) describes *breviramea* as a "tree of narrow pyramidal habit, with short branches: branchlets crowded, glossy green on both sides." More recent authors have reduced *breviramea* to synonymy with the species (Ohwi, 1984). To use this essentially botanical name to describe the bonsai hinokis is inappropriate since 'Chabo-hiba' is clearly a horticultural variety that has been in cultivation in Japan since the 1700's.
5. The name *nana* was first published by E.-A. Carrier in 1867 as, "much smaller than the species, this variety is distinguished mostly by its branches, branchlets and twigs which are very slender and very short." In the 1904 S. M. Nursery Company auction catalogue, 'Chabo-hiba' is listed as synonymous with *Thuja obtusa nanus*. In 1918, E.H. Wilson of the Arnold Arboretum visited the Yokohama Nursery Company and photographed its specimens of 'Chabo-hiba,' which he labeled *Chamaecyparis obtusa* var. *nana*. Since this name does not accurately describe 'Chabo-hiba,' it should be rejected.

Acknowledgments

The author would like to thank Dr. John Creech, former Director of the U.S. National Arboretum, for information concerning Unger and Boehmer; Mr. Barry Yinger, Head of the Horticulture Department, Somerset County Park Commission, for providing the author with a copy of *Somoku Kihin Kagami*; Mr. Hitoshi Kanegae of New England Bonsai Gardens for his help with the Japanese language; István Rácz for taking the pictures of the Larz Anderson Collection; and the Library of the Arnold Arboretum for keeping the Yokohama Nursery catalogues for all those years. A generous grant from the Arnold Arboretum Associates was helpful in funding the publication of this work.

References

Anderson, I. 1937. *Japanese dwarf trees collected by the Hon. Larz Anderson.* Typed manuscript in the Archives of the Arnold Arboretum.

Anderson, I. 1940. *Larz Anderson, Letters and Journals of a Diplomat.* New York: Fleming H. Revell Co.

Beissner, L. 1900. Interessantes uber coniferen. *Mitt. Deutsch. Dend. Gesell.* 9: 57–69.

Brickell, C.D., et al. 1980. International code of nomenclature for cultivated plants. *Regnum Vegetabile* 104.

Carrier, E.-A. 1867. *Traite General des Conifereres,* 2nd ed. Paris: Chez L'Auteur.

Carrier, E.-A. 1889. Japonaiseries. *Revue Horticole* 61: 374–378.

Creech, J. 1988. Pioneer plantsmen in Japan. *The Garden* 113(8): 380–383.

Derderian, C. E. 1971. Japanese theory—American practice. *Arnoldia* 31: 294–296.

Derderian, C. E. 1980. Bonsai at the Arnold Arboretum. *Bonsai Jour.* 13(4): 75–78.

Downing. A. J. 1841. *A Treatise on the Theory and Practice of Landscape Gardening.* New York: Orange Judd Co.

The gardens at Weld. 1904. *Town and Country* 59(1): 12–16.

Gordon, G. 1875. *The Pinetum,* new ed. London: Henry G. Bohn.

Guthrie, E. 1933. The ancient art of bonsai. *House Beautiful* 73 (5): 284 F–N.

Harada, J. 1928. *The Gardens of Japan.* London: The Studio Ltd.

Hornibrook, M. 1938. *Dwarf and Slow-Growing Conifers.* 2nd ed. Reprint 1973. Little Compton, R.I.: Theophrastus.

Kintaro. 1827. *Somoku Kihin Kagami.* 3 vols. Reprinted in facsimile in 1976. Tokyo: Seiseido (in Japanese).

Koreshoff, D. R. 1984. *Bonsai: Its Art, Science, History and Philosophy.* Brisbane: Boolarong.

Kurata, S., et al. 1971. *Illustrated Important Forest Trees of Japan.* Tokyo: Chikyo Shuppan Co.

Long, C. R. 1971. An informal history of bonsai. *Arnoldia* 31: 261–273.

Masters, M.T. 1881. On the conifers of Japan. *Jour. Linn. Soc.* 18: 473–524.

Maumené, A. 1902. *Les Arbres Nains Japonair.* Paris: Francois Tedesca.

Ohwi, J. 1984. *Flora of Japan.* Washington, D.C.: Smithsonian Institution.

Rehder, A. 1914. *Chamaecyparis,* in *The Standard Cyclopedia of Horticulture,* L. H. Bailey, ed. New York: Macmillan.

Spingarn, J. W. 1978. The Baldwin dwarfs. *Bull. Am. Rock Gard. Soc.* 36(1): 123–125.

Tsukamoto, Y., et al. 1976. *Explanation Volume to Accompany 1976 Facsimile Reprint of Somoku Kihin Kagami.* Tokyo: Seiseido (in Japanese).

Unger, A. 1930. Japan –betrachtungen und –erinnerungen. *Die Gardenwelt* 34(2): 25–26.

Walker, E. H. 1976. *Flora of Okinawa and the Southern Ryukyu Islands.* Washington, D.C.: Smithsonian Institution.

Wyman, D. 1938. The Larz Anderson collection of Japanese dwarf trees. *Arnold Arb. Bull. Pop. Info.,* ser. 4, vol. 6: 31–39.

Wyman, D. 1964. Bonsai at the Arnold Arboretum. *Arnoldia* 24 (12): 101–104.

Yoshio, T., and O. Motoyoshi. 1891. *Yuyo Shokubutsu Zusetsu.* 3 vols. Tokyo: Japanese Imperial Museum.

Yoshimura, Y., and G. M. Halford. 1957. *The Japanese Art of Miniature Trees and Landscapes.* Rutland, Vt.: Charles E. Tuttle.

Young, D.S. 1985. *Bonsai: The Art and Technique.* Englewood Cliffs, N.J.:Prentice-Hall.

Portraits of the Larz Anderson Collection 1913–1989

Acer buergerianum, Trident Maple (#870-37), started in 1852. **Top left**, the plant c. 1913, 58 cm high (23 in). **Bottom left**, the plant in 1933. **Above**, the plant in 1989, 70 cm high (28 in). Photo by Rácz and Debreczy. Note how the plant has remained in the same container for over 75 years.

Chamaecyparis obtusa 'Chabo-hiba,' Compact Hinoki Cypress (#892-49), started in 1787. **Left**, the plant in 1952. Notice how the branches are tied to bamboo sticks to hold them in a horizontal position. **Above**, the plant in 1989, 160 cm wide (63 in). Photo by Rácz and Debreczy.

Chamaecyparis obtusa 'Chabo-hiba,' Compact Hinoki Cypress (#880-37), started in 1832. **Top left**, the plant in 1954. **Bottom left**, the plant in 1963. **Above**, the plant in 1989, 70 cm high (28 in). Photo by Rácz and Debreczy. This unusual boat-shaped container is original and may well have been a gift to the Andersons, a "travelling bonsai," when they left Japan in 1913.

Prunus subhirtella, Higan Cherry (#889-37), started in 1852. **Bottom left**, the plant c. 1913, 61 cm high (24 in). **Top left**, the plant in 1965. Note the same pot as in 1913. **Above**, the plant in 1989, 50 cm high (20 in). Photo by Rácz and Debreczy.

Chamaecyparis obtusa 'Chabo-hiba', Compact Hinoki Cypress. (#879-37), started in 1802. **Top left**, the plant in 1963. **Above**, the final result of a successful operation performed by Connie Derderian in 1969. As she describes it, "A lower branch had split away from the main trunk of 879-37. Rather than cut it off and lose it, a wedge-shaped piece of soil was cut away from the root ball to create a new plant. It was put into the container on the right." **Bottom left**, the lower branch (#101-69) in 1989, 60 cm wide (24 in). Photo by Rácz and Debreczy.

Pinus parviflora, Japanese White Pine (#893-49), started in 1887. **Left**, the plant in 1952. Note how bamboo sticks were used in training the branches. **Above**, the plant in 1989, 100 cm high (39 in). Photo by Rácz and Debreczy.

Chamaecyparis obtusa 'Chabo-hiba,' Compact Hinoki Cypress (#878-37), started in 1787. **Top left**, the plant in 1938. **Bottom left**, the plant in 1954. **Above**, the plant in 1989, 120 cm high (47 in). Photo by Rácz and Debreczy. Note how the curved branch to the lower left of the plant has remained a constant feature over time.

APPENDIX

Bonsai Maintenance at Yokohama Nursery

The Arnold Arboretum is fortunate to have in its library the catalogues issued by the Yokohama Nursery Company between the years 1901 and 1922. Interestingly they all contain exactly the same instructions for how to take care of the dwarf plants that the nursery sold. This information has great historical significance since it is one of the earliest English descriptions of how to maintain the health of bonsai plants. The instructions are reprinted below in their entirety. According to Dr. John Creech, these instructions could well have been written by Alfred Unger's American wife, Mary, who published two books on Japanese plants around 1898.

Dwarfed Trees Growing in Jardinieres and Their Cultural Direction

Treatment of *Thuja obtusa* [= *Chamaecyparis obtusa*]. During spring and summer, by preference keep this plant in a sunny airy situation where the wind will pass freely through the branches; water once a day giving just enough to make the soil moist; in dry hot weather it may be necessary to give water twice a day. Care however should be taken not to have the soil wet and never water unless the plant needs it. Watering overhead in dry weather is bad but rain is always beneficial. During winter keep the tree in a cold greenhouse partially shaded, or in an unheated orangery, giving water about once in 10 days; the soil however must never be allowed to get dry. (The science of successful culture of all plants in pots consists in judicious watering, giving too much or too little is equally bad.)

Treated as above this plant is very ornamental on balconies, terraces, etc. If this plant is kept indoors, it should always be placed out-of-doors at night and as often as it is not wanted for decoration. Indoors it should never be exposed to the dry heat from a stove or open fireplace, otherwise the leaves will drop off and the plant perish.

Pinus pentaphylla [= *Pinus parviflora*] and pine trees in general growing in jardinieres require the same attention in watering and general treatment as *Thuja obtusa* but are not so much influenced by atmospheric conditions; nevertheless sun and air are necessary to maintain health, therefore keep the plants out-of-doors as much as possible.

Maples and other deciduous trees take the same treatment as *Thuja obtusa* as regards watering, but are much more accommodating than evergreens; in fairly mild climates the maples may remain out-of-doors all winter, but where the frost is very severe they should be kept in a cool cellar after the leaves have fallen in autumn; the soil must always be kept moist but not *wet*; early in spring put the plants out-of-doors and fully exposed to all weathers and when in full leaf use for decoration indoors as needed.

MANURING: When the trees commence growing in spring, we give manure twice a month, say March, April, May and June, again September and October. In the hot days of July and August, we give no manure and the same in winter and early spring, the plants then being at rest; the best manure is finely powdered oil cake or bone meal. To a jardiniere one foot in diameter we give 3 or 4 large teaspoonfuls *not heaped* of this dry manure spread evenly around the edge of the jardiniere; a larger or smaller jardiniere will require more or less. For a small jardiniere, say three inches by six inches, half a teaspoonful will be ample each time.

REPOTTING: This is done by us once in two or three years as follows; lift the plant out of the jardiniere and with a sharp pointed stick remove about one-third of the old soil around the *edges and bottom*, cutting away a portion of the *old fine* roots but none of the strong roots, then replace the plant in the same jardiniere first looking to the drainage; for a small shallow jardiniere we use a flat piece of tin or a flat crock over each hole; over this spread some rich fresh soil; neatly balance the plant and fill up with the same rich fresh soil to within one-half an inch of the rim; this holds the water and prevents the manure being washed over the sides of the jardiniere; also the soil should be made sufficiently tight round the edges of the jardiniere to prevent the escape of water, it being of the first importance that the entire ball of soil around the plant be moistened at each watering. Should the watering of the plant at any time be neglected and the soil has become quite dry, put the jardiniere in a tub of water for 10 or 15 minutes, *not longer*, and if the injury is not too serious, the plant will recover. In the case of large plants, we use hollow crocks for drainage, the same as is used by growers of specimen plants. After several repottings, the plant having increased in size, shift into a larger pot, but as dwarfness is the thing aimed at, the smaller the shift the better. Repotting should be done in February or March just before spring growth commences.

We advise when it is possible to get the above work done by a good gardener who has been accustomed to the handling of heaths, New Holland plants, etc. In the case of *very* shallow jardinieres we find it desirable annually to replace a portion of the old soil to maintain a healthy growth.

PRUNING: To maintain dwarfness in the trees, pinch back the young growth; this we usually do from April to the middle of June and always with the finger and thumb, a practice followed by the late Mr. Thomas Rivers of Sawbridgeworth, England, when preparing his dwarfed fruit trees fruiting in pots. In *Thuja obtusa* we pinch out the points of the young growth all over the plant to maintain the form; this practice we also apply to *Cryptomeria* and all other conifers except *Pinus*. *Pinus*: we pinch out the points of the irregular growth simply to maintain the shape of the plant. Pomegranate, *Lagerstroemia indica*, flowering peach, flowering cherry, etc.: we pinch back *the nonflowering* shoots either before or after blooming. Wisteria: in July and August we pinch back all the young growth leaving only four or five leaves on each shoot. Maple and other deciduous trees are pinched back at the same time as *Thuja obtusa* leaving two to four leaves as may be necessary to maintain the desired shape of the plants. Should a second growth be made, the same rule is followed of pinching out the points.

40

Larz Anderson